UNFOLDING POTENTIAL

UNFOLDING POTENTIAL

A JEWISH JOURNEY OF SELF-DEVELOPMENT

JONAH S.C. MUSKAT-BROWN, MSW

Mosaica Press, Inc.

Copyright © 2016 by Mosaica Press

Designed and typeset by Rayzel Broyde

All rights reserved

ISBN 13: 978-1-937887-84-1   ISBN 10: 1-937887-84-7

All rights reserved. No part of this book may be used or reproduced or transmitted in any form or by any means, electronic or mechanical, including photocopying, recording, or by any information storage and retrieval system, without written permission from the publisher.

Published and distributed by:

Mosaica Press, Inc.

www.mosaicapress.com

info@mosaicapress.com

Jonah Simcha Chaim Muskat-Brown has compiled a beautiful collection of original thoughts — on Torah, *Yiddishkeit*, *Yamim Tovim*, relationships, and so much more.

Jonah Simcha Chaim is a wonderful person and an exceptionally caring, giving, and loving *eved Hashem*. His creative writing and insightful, soaring *divrei Torah* reflect his unique nature and generous, searching spirit.

I enjoy reading and sharing his Torah, and bless him to continue spreading the warmth and sweetness of Judaism with *Am Yisrael* and the world!

Rabbi Judah Mischel
Executive Director
Founder, Tzama Nafshi

RABBI DR. TZVI HERSH WEINREB
Executive Vice President, Emeritus

212.613.8264 *tel*
212.613.0635 *fax*
execthw@ou.org *email*

ELEVEN BROADWAY | NEW YORK, NY 10004-1303
212.563.4000 | info@ou.org | www.ou.org

May 2, 2016/24 Nisan 5776

I have read the book *Unfolding Potential* by Jonah Simcha Chaim Muskat-Brown. The theme of the book is human potential, a topic that has long been my abiding interest in working with people. The author elaborates upon this important theme within the context of the major festivals of the Jewish calendar.

As I read the book, I was constantly reminded of one of my favorite sayings, attributed to the German philosopher Goethe: "If you treat a person as he is, he will remain as he is. If you treat him as he ought to be and could be, he will become as he ought to be and could be." Mr. Muskat-Brown succeeds in encouraging all of us all to become what we ought to be and can be. He is to be congratulated for this inspiring work.

Rabbi Dr. Tzvi Hersh Weinreb

Founded in 1898 as the Union of Orthodox Jewish Congregations of America
איחוד קהילות האורתודוקסים באמריקה

In Jonah Simcha Chaim Muskat-Brown's innovative work, he leads the reader on an exploration of who they are, and more importantly, who they can become. His writing shows the power of internalizing and personalizing Torah concepts — arguably a prerequisite to true personal growth and development. Jonah is an individual who dedicates his life to helping others reveal their abilities, and his own life has proved how hard work, focus, and unwavering faith can allow one to accomplish the unimaginable. I hope this work will be taken to heart by all those who read it, and that it will be the impetus in helping unfold that potential that exists within each and every one of us.

Rebbetzin Sara Esther Crispe
Co-Founder
Founder of JewishWoman.org
World-renowned speaker

It has been a pleasure and a true *kavod* to see how much Jonah Simcha Chaim Muskat-Brown has grown in his personal journey. His unshakable *emunah* in the *Ribbono shel Olam* and in His Torah can be found in much of this inspiring book. *Divrei Chassidus* and modern psychology are interwoven here to try and portray the complex tapestry of human life and the intricate, thoughtful, and empowering Jewish calendar.

I wish him much *hatzlachah* and a huge *yashar koach* for this endeavor. May Jonah Simcha Chaim's journey continue for many years.

Rabbi Aaron Greenberg
Canadian director
Orthodox Union/Jewish Learning Initiative on Campus (OU/JLIC)

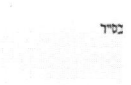

Rabbi Yehoshua Weber
rabbi

Rabbi Yitzchok Kerzner
rabbi emeritus

May 4, 2016

כו ניסן תשע"ו

I have known Jonah Simcha Chaim Muskat Brown for a number of years and have been inspired by Jonah's development in Torah and as a social worker.

I have also had the privilege of reading and reviewing Jonah's inspiring book. In his work, Jonah melds penetrating knowledge of classic Torah sources and training in psychology and social work. Jonah uses both Torah and psychology as lanterns that penetrate the recesses of our inner souls and observe sides of ourselves that, in all likelihood, we have never encountered. We come face to face with our fears and our weaknesses, but also our hopes and our potentialities, and are stronger and better off because of it.

Jonah's takes the disparate parts of our inner and outer selves, the familial, the social, the religious and the financial and creates a whole – and a thought process – infinitely greater than its disparate parts.

I commend Jonah for a well written work. May הקב"ה give him the wherewithal to continue inspiring his patients, his readers, all of כלל ישראל and the world at large.

יהושע יוחנן וועבער

11 Lowesmoor Avenue
Toronto, On M3H 3H6
416-633-4193

clantonpark.com

TABLE OF CONTENTS

Acknowledgments	13
Introduction: The Onset of Potential	15
The Potential to Be Different: Rosh Hashanah	19
On Teshuvah and Defense Mechanisms: Yom Kippur	26
Happiness as a State of Becoming: Sukkos	31
To Kindle a Flame Buried Within: Chanukah	38
Active Choosing: Purim Katan	44
Potential Actualized: Purim	50
The Journey: From Purim to Pesach	56
The Potential to Love: Pesach	62
Becoming Whole Again: Shavuos	69
Mending the Brokenness: The Three Weeks and Tishah b'Av	74
A Never-Ending Story	78
Appendix	79
About the Author	89

ACKNOWLEDGMENTS

To my parents and siblings — for believing in me when so many others did not. For being the greatest teachers of the art of self-actualization: never allowing me to give up on myself and always pushing me to unlock further aspects of my potential.

To the very special and holy campers of Camp HASC — for teaching me what it means to be a part of something much larger than myself and for inspiring me to use my creativity to make things happen when so many others said they couldn't.

To my *rebbeim*, *rebbetzins*, mentors, and colleagues — for always being there when I need someone to talk to, share ideas with, and ask for guidance. For inspiring me, educating me, and continuously being positive and healthy role models. And for teaching me what true *ahavas Yisrael* looks like and what it means to be a true *shaliach* for *kedushah*.

To my *chavrusos*, students, and clients — for sharing Torah, challenging me, and inspiring me to think and teach outside the box.

To my readers — for reading my Torah over the years, challenging my ideas, and offering feedback. And for encouraging me to transform my Torah into book form.

To the staff of Mosaica Press — for their constant and professional support, encouragement, and guidance from the very onset of this project.

To the *Ribbono shel Olam* — for opening up so many gates for me. For inspiring me to complete this project and for providing me with the skills to bring it from the realm of abstract thought into the practical.

INTRODUCTION: THE ONSET OF POTENTIAL

What Is Potential?

Potential is an inherent aspect of each of us that remains, for the most part, a mystery. Potential is a drive (and an ability) that allows each of us to succeed — but is not the end result of that success. According to Aristotle,[1] it enables one to transform into that which he is capable of becoming, allowing a person or object to become more whole than his (or its) current state. For Abraham Maslow,[2] "What a man *can* be, he *must* be"; fulfilling our potential is what leads to ultimate happiness[3] and inner peace.[4]

When does potential begin to appear?

Perhaps potential begins shortly prior to birth. A fetus rests peacefully within its mother's womb, passively receiving nourishment that will allow it to express itself as it exits and begins its development in the outside world.

Or, perhaps potential lies in the hands of parents and teachers who help shape and educate the child. As he learns new skills throughout life, he becomes better able to apply himself and his capabilities toward that which he sets out to conquer.

---

1   Aristotle, *The Metaphysics*, trans. H. Lawson-Tancred (London/New York: Penguin Classics, 1999), 253–282.
2   Well-known for his Hierarchy of Needs, first presented in 1943.
3   Abraham Harold Maslow, "A Theory of Human Motivation," *Psychological Review* 50, no.4 (1943): 370–396.
4   Joseph Sassoon, *Self-Actualization: Theory and Technology* (Montreal: Humanica Press, 1988), preface and p. xii.

How to Develop Potential

But what if potential had no beginning? What if it were an aspect of each of us that constantly develops over time?[5]

However and whenever it begins, as we will see, potential is something to be nurtured. True, we each receive various abilities at birth, but it ultimately remains up to each of us to bring them to fruition as we continue our lives.

How do we develop these abilities? How do we fulfill our potential? We are not alone and directionless in the most central of life's challenges. Judaism (and each of the holidays, in particular) offers us some of the greatest guidance on how to actualize aspects of ourselves. Whether it is the potential for resilience, forgiveness, happiness, love, or unity, each serve as an opportunity to learn more about ourselves and how we can better interact with the world around us. Unlike a skill that we can be taught, potential lies within each of us and is waiting to be nurtured and brought to the forefront.

Potential Is Highly Individual

But perhaps the greatest component of the definition of "potential" is that it belongs and is unique to each person. Striving to be like another may be empowering, but we cannot allow it to distract us from striving to reach the potentials we are each capable of. Potential is not something that remains stagnant. And because our various potentials never remain the same throughout life, we each have the awesome gift of choosing to be different with each passing day — becoming more wholesome and reaching heights we never thought possible.

The Journey of Potential

Potential is a journey. It is a blessing bestowed upon each of us from Above, but lies in our hands alone to bring to the forefront throughout our lives.

At times, the roads that lie ahead are bumpy. At times, they are smooth.

---

5   Psychologists and social workers divide the human lifespan into multiple stages of growth, in which individuals further actualize aspects of themselves as they develop over time.

The most important thing to remember is to never to give up. Though we may occasionally doubt ourselves and our abilities, our Maker does not. He believes in us and the accomplishments He knows each of us is capable of.

Studying the art of potential and self-actualization requires that we ask ourselves not *what*, but *who*. Who am I and who am I able to become? The focus is not necessarily on the things we have done (though they are important), but more so on the selves we are and can become over time.

1

THE POTENTIAL TO BE DIFFERENT: ROSH HASHANAH

The Cycles of Repetition

"Pointless, everything is pointless!" writes King Solomon, the wisest of all men, in his Ecclesiastes.

> What profit do people attain in their toil under the sun? A generation passes on and another is born, but the earth will endure forever; the sun rises and the sun sets, yet it returns to its initial place only to rise again. Going to the south and to the north, the wind blows around and around only to revisit its initial starting point. All the rivers flow into the sea, but the sea does not become full — and from where they have come, so too will they flow once more.[1]

In his *Nesivos Sholom*,[2] the Slonimer Rebbe analyzes Rosh Hashanah against the bulk of the other holidays mentioned in *Parshas Emor*.[3] He teaches that unlike Pesach (with its matzah), Shavuos (with its *shtei halechem*), and Sukkos (with its mitzvah of dwelling in the *sukkah* and taking the *lulav and esrog*), Rosh Hashanah seems to have no real focal point (or mitzvah). This is how the verse describes it: "In the seventh month, on the first of the month, there shall be a day of rest for you, a remembrance [with] shofar blasts..."[4] True, there is a mitzvah to hear

---

1 Ecclesiastes 1:1–7.
2 *Nesivos Sholom*, Rosh Hashanah, first discourse.
3 Leviticus 23.
4 Ibid. 23:24.

the shofar on the day, but the Torah does not reveal that more explicitly until later on.[5] It seems, as its name suggests, that Rosh Hashanah is but another beginning to something that has already been.

A question comes to mind: if Rosh Hashanah is the beginning of something that already was, what is that initial phenomenon that we are called upon to commemorate? To answer this, the *Nesivos Sholom* relies on one of the central verses from the Rosh Hashanah prayers: "*Zeh ha-yom techilas ma'asecha, zikaron l'yom rishon* — This is the day of the beginning of your doing, a remembrance of the first day." But Rosh Hashanah is not a celebration of the anniversary of the creation of the world; G-d began Creation on 25 Elul, five days prior! Rosh Hashanah is the anniversary of the creation of humankind — the species, which the Sages teach was the focal point of Creation, the purpose behind G-d's creating heaven and earth.[6]

The Potential for Renewal

The Arizal[7] teaches that all of G-d's creations are renewed each year on the condition that they have lived up to their creative purpose. But what is the purpose of our creation? What are each of us supposed to be living up to that we may merit renewal?

G-d, as explained in the *Midrash*,[8] desired a *dirah b'tachtonim*, a dwelling place within the lower worlds.[9] Humankind, created in the image and likeness of its Maker,[10] is the only creation capable of bringing about and preparing such a place. While all of creation continues to exist because of a divine vitality flowing into its many facets, only human beings are capable of utilizing that vitality for both physical purposes and higher and more refined pursuits. Whereby the solar system, plant, and animal kingdoms are passively given renewal (*isarusa d'l'eila*), humanity is endowed with the potential to transform itself and its environment into vessels for G-dliness and to accept such nourishment (*isarusa d'l'sata*).

---

5 Numbers 29:1.
6 *Vayikra Rabbah* 14:1.
7 Referred to by the *Nesivos Sholom*.
8 *Tanchuma, Naso* 7:1.
9 Tanya 36.
10 Genesis 1:26.

The question awaiting us each year is whether we are living up to this task, and if not, how can we do better? Are we merely "being" or are we transcending the status quo of being? Will we allow another year to come and pass, or will we devote ourselves within that coming year to bringing about more revealed goodness?

The Freedom to Be Different

Because G-d is completely free, human beings — created in His image and likeness — also possess freedom (to the obvious extent that they are finite creatures). Out of all His many possible adjectives, G-d tells Moses to convince the Jewish people of His greatness by using the description *Ehyeh asher Ehyeh* (oftentimes translated as, "I will be that which I will be").[11] Perhaps the awesomeness in this description does not simply lie in G-d being so transcendent that finite beings cannot comprehend Him, but that because He is free, He is fully capable of being that which He *chooses* to be.

G-dliness itself, therefore, is the courage to be free – to reject the limitations on who we can become. To be free means to be nonconforming and unpredictable, constantly different today from yesterday and tomorrow from today.[12]

In societies of the ancient world, life was solar-based and consistent: the sun would rise and set, only to repeat this again the following day. The ancient world consisted of cultures that valued several gods, each operating in and limited by the natural world. Individuals would die and be born, each within their social class and confined to a pre-destined, Oedipean[13] drama of life.

Different Generation, Same Calling

Perhaps this is the beauty in how Moses gave over his final legacy to the Jewish nation and the world. As the Torah comes to a close, he summons

---

11 Exodus 3:14.
12 Jonathan Sacks, *Future Tense* (New York: Schocken Books, 2009), 231–252.
13 Oedipus is a character in Greek mythology, who, by prophecy of an oracle, was destined from birth to ultimately murder his father and marry his mother. The more he tried to escape this prophecy, the more it became fulfilled.

the people and instructs them that every seven years, the king of that generation is to gather them once again and read to them from the scroll of the Torah (this mitzvah is known as *Hakhel*).[14] In other words, every seven years, they are to renew their covenant and reconnect to their divine calling. Essentially, this is their way of recommitting to their relationship with G-d and His Torah, akin to a couple rewriting their wedding vows several years after their initial wedding. Indeed, this should be done daily (as we read in the *Shema*),[15] but also more formally during specific times of the year, as well.

Why not just continue doing what we are doing? Why the need for renewal?

Religious stagnation is not a fulfillment of our potential, but rather the opposite. For Judaism to survive, it must continuously be revived and made personally meaningful for each individual and within each generation. True, the messages of the Torah that were issued to the generations of yesteryear are a calling to live a sacred life, but they also call out to be renewed daily in the present. They call on each of us to dare to be different, dare to grow, and dare to be better than others (and oftentimes we ourselves) thought us capable of.

Perhaps this was the genius behind Carl Rogers' Person- (or Client-) Centered Therapy[16] — a theory positing that each individual has hidden potentials waiting to be unleashed, if only he is given the means and encouragement to discover how much he is truly capable of accomplishing.

Moses' final calling, and perhaps our first, is to write down the song of the Torah and teach its melody to his people. Speech is finite, definitive, and restrictive. Moses taught that the Torah is not a stagnant, cyclical manual. Rather, it is both divine and *alive* in a sense: a magnificent work of musical art in which each generation and each individual has the responsibility of adding his own note to the symphony of his people. This is why Judaism is so vastly different from any other peoples' way of life: since its

---

14 Deuteronomy 31:10.
15 Ibid. 6:4–9; Ibid. 11:13–21.
16 Carl Rogers, "Significant Aspects of Client-Centered Therapy," *American Psychologist* 1, no. 10 (1946): 415–422.

story is constantly being written, its end is always yet to come[17] — waiting for each of us to author our own narratives.

Becoming

While Rosh Hashanah is indeed a day of judgment, this is not its focus. The *Nesivos Sholom* points out that the prayers of the *Yom Tov* center not on G-d's judgment of His creations, but rather largely on their appointing Him as King. This is why, he teaches, the prophet Nehemiah told the people, "Today [Rosh Hashanah] is a holy day for G-d, do not mourn…Go eat rich foods and drink sweet beverages and send to those who have no preparations, because today is a holy day for G-d — do not be sad."[18] Rosh Hashanah is future-driven. It is focused not so much on our past mistakes and how G-d might judge us for what we did (or did not do) correctly, but more so on how we choose to conduct ourselves in the present and the types of people we strive to become in the future. The Jewish story, of which we are each a part, is one that is constantly being written.

Rabbi Simcha Bunim of Peshischa[19] tells a story about one of the Baal Shem Tov's lengthy journeys, in which he would miraculously arrive more quickly than expected. On one such occasion, the Baal Shem Tov had to embark on a lengthy journey and borrowed strong horses and a wagon for the trip. Accustomed to traveling for long periods of time, the horses assumed that they would be stopped every so often to be given food and to rest. To their amazement, they found themselves traveling with no need for food, and passing all the usual rest stops. Perhaps, they speculated to themselves, they had transformed into human beings and would soon rest at the human stops that followed the animal resting areas. As they passed the human stops as well, the horses further hypothesized that perhaps they had, in fact, turned into angels and no longer possessed the physical needs for rest or food. Upon arriving at the Baal Shem Tov's destination, however, the horses were led into a

---

17 Sacks, *Future Tense*, 240.
18 Nehemiah 8:9–10.
19 DovBer Pinson, *Reclaiming the Self: On the Pathway of Teshuvah* (Brooklyn: IYYUN Publishing, 2011), 67–68.

stable, where they found mounds of hay awaiting them, and they began devouring it, as horses are wont to do.

By partaking in holiness for a while, the Peshischa Rebbe teaches, we run the risk of forgetting our true purpose and thinking of ourselves as angels. How do we test whether we are going through mere cycles or whether we are transcending our "natural" selves? The best indication is how we approach that to which we are accustomed from years past. Do we devour whatever we face in life like the horses in the story had initially learned and expected to do, or do we transform our old habits into fresh behaviors that allow for personal growth and increased holiness?

The Language of Potential

A year has come and passed, and another awaits. The sun will once again set and rise the following morning. Will tomorrow be different, or merely a repetition of what was accomplished today? Who will learn to speak the language of potential and thus "live"? Who will remain stuck in the past and thus "die"? Who will act within nature, and who will strive to transcend time and overcome his nature — thereby choosing against the status quo and focusing on nourishing his truest self?

The choice is open to each and every one of us — and we are called upon to choose life![20]

---

20 Deuteronomy 30:19.

QUESTIONS FOR REFLECTION

- Are the consistent habits and behaviors that I have created for myself beneficial or detrimental to the life I currently, or desire to, live?

- Is there one area in my life (or my day or week) that I can transform to allow for freshness?

2

ON TESHUVAH AND DEFENSE MECHANISMS: YOM KIPPUR

Who Are We?

Teshuvah is a call to change oneself, to turn around and begin living life afresh, with a new perspective of reality. That already is huge — but can it be something greater? At its depth, *teshuvah* is the process of looking into the core of who we are and seeing the untarnished soul buried within.

The *Midrash*[1] relates that G-d, wisdom, prophecy, and the Torah all gathered to discuss what ought to be done with one who transgresses:

- Wisdom, relying on the words of King Solomon — the wisest of all men — brings a supporting text: "Evil shall pursue one who transgresses."[2]

- Prophecy offers an answer from the Book of Ezekiel: "The soul who transgresses shall perish."[3]

- The Torah comments: "[One who transgresses] should bring a guilt-offering and he will be forgiven."

- Finally, G-d steps forward and replies, "[Let one who transgresses] do *teshuvah* and he will be forgiven."

---

1 *Yalkut Shimoni*, Psalms 25, *remez* 432.
2 *Mishlei* 13:21.
3 Ezekiel 18:4.

One with G-d

Each answer can be viewed as a paradigm for how we live our lives:

- The first approach follows the laws of cause and effect, which dictate that the ways in which we behave have consequences. One who commits evil adds additional negativity to the world which will ultimately rebound and affect him in return.

- In the second perspective, the realm of prophecy, there exists no room for anything other than goodness. To receive prophecy, an individual must prepare himself spiritually to a point where he comes close to reaching an angelic state of being. The mind of the prophet is beyond the realm of wisdom. All that exists in life, essentially, is spirituality and goodness. It is not enough that the sinner is punished with his own rebounded negativity; he must cease to exist completely.

- Continuing, the Torah was given to us with the understanding that we will each make mistakes throughout our lives. Akin to a doctor's prescription for medication, the Torah is our guidebook for elevated living. According to the third perspective, when we slip, we are given the opportunity to rectify ourselves by bringing a sacrifice to atone for our errors. Life must always be lived with a sense of balance: when we partake in negativity, we must make amends by performing acts of positivity.

- Lastly, G-d Himself declares that if we desire closeness, all we need to do is engage in *teshuvah* and we can attain it. True, life should include cause and effect, and yes, reality must be lived with the goal of harmony, but *teshuvah* transcends nature. With *teshuvah*, we return to the selves we initially were prior to making a particular mistake. We return to our *neshamah*, which is a piece of G-d, and we become one with G-d again by recommitting to His ways and recommitting to a life of holiness (to which the *neshamah* is accustomed).[4]

---

4   Pinson, *Reclaiming the Self*.

Teshuvah and the Soul

Teshuvah touches and reveals the essence of each of us: our *neshamos*, our souls. Each morning upon rising, we declare — and are meant to recognize — that the soul which G-d gave us remains pure and untarnished. This deep truth has some important implications:

To forgive another means to look into his soul and see that it shares the same root-source[5] as our own. To forgive ourselves means to accept that the behaviors we exhibit externally are not always accurate representations of our truest selves buried within. As we develop in life, we collect various garments known as defense mechanisms that we employ to protect our emotional wellbeing. Each garment acts as a shield for our inner holiness, progressively concealing our raw and vulnerable selves from being fully exposed — a process, which *Kabbalah* teaches, mirrors the act of Creation. Deep within, our souls remain unconditionally beautiful and pure.

Unchanged and Untarnished

In the beginning, only G-d existed. He desired a partner (i.e., humankind) to help complete His works of Creation,[6] but could not create a finite being capable of existing alongside His infiniteness. Therefore, He "contracted" Himself, so to speak, and concealed His essence, layer by layer, to the point where physical reality and humankind were able to coexist alongside His greatness.[7] G-d's essence remained unaltered, just as our deepest essence remains in a constant state of holiness, but He limited His revelation to allow room for those who were not like Him. Had G-d allowed His raw essence to be revealed in its fullest glory at all times, we would be overwhelmed and perish.

Protecting the Self

On a different level, the same occurs within each of us. To achieve success in the physical world, we "cover up" our real selves and develop

---

5 Each Jewish soul is a direct fragment of G-d (Tanya 2), and we each continuously received vitality from that shared Source.
6 *Shabbos* 119b.
7 Tanya 21:48–49.

various tactics to protect our egos, so as to allow ourselves to function (and excel) in life. Whether at work or in our interpersonal relationships, we would not be able to succeed if we allowed our raw, vulnerable, and pure selves to constantly be exposed. Indeed, we reveal more intimate aspects of ourselves to those with whom we feel close on special occasions, but for the most part, we know full well to protect those facets of our being that are most fragile. Because covering up our "real" selves is, sadly, a large part of daily life, we easily forget that our outer persona is *not* who we *truly* are. *Teshuvah* is the act of returning to who we are beneath those protective covers. We pull back our personal layers and clean out the "dirt" that has accumulated over the previous year. This is why we refrain from physicality to such an extent on Yom Kippur: to help us focus on the pure, inner essence of who we are — our *neshamah*. After a judgment-filled Rosh Hashanah and a subsequent week of reflection leading up to Yom Kippur, for just one day we feel close enough to G-d that we are comfortable exposing who we truly are and the inner child buried within.[8]

Vulnerability Exposed

Yom Kippur is not as much about judgment as it is about closeness. Just as the soul has five ascending levels,[9] so too do our prayers on Yom Kippur consist of five *tefillos* — as if to remind us that however low we think we may have fallen, when we reconnect (or for some, connect for the first time) with our inner essence, we can soar.

Achas b'shanah, once a year,[10] Yom Kippur allows each of us the opportunity to transcend the reasoning of our intellect — dictating how undeserving we are — and realize that no matter how soiled our garments have become, we can always remove the outer layers of dirt and find our authentic selves buried within. No matter how deep a diamond falls into the mud, it still remains a diamond.

---

8 The "inner child" is that aspect of ourselves which remains genuine and pure, regardless of our development through life. As we age, however, we create various defense mechanisms which allow us to embrace the so-called "adult" world in which we live, thereby covering up and protecting this part of our being.
9 *Bereishis Rabbah* 14:9.
10 Leviticus 16:34.

QUESTIONS FOR REFLECTION

- With whom do I feel most comfortable revealing my truest and most vulnerable self? How often does this occur?

- Am I the one to initiate forgiveness or do I wait until someone who has hurt me asks to be forgiven?

- How often do I forgive myself? Do I make time in my day (or week) to get to know the authentic "me" buried within?

3

HAPPINESS AS A STATE OF BECOMING: SUKKOS

The Time of Our Happiness

There is something confusing about how we refer to the holiday of Sukkos:

- Pesach is known as *z'man cheruseinu*,[1] the time of our freedom, which seems logical since the Jewish nation was miraculously redeemed from Egypt at that time.

- Shavuos, known as *z'man matan Toraseinu*,[2] the time of the giving of the Torah, seems reasonable as well, because it was at this time that the Jewish people accepted the Torah and collectively entered into a covenant with G-d.

- Sukkos, however, is referred to as *z'man simchaseinu*,[3] the time of our happiness.

What does this happiness refer to? According to the Talmud,[4] the *sukkah*-huts of the festival have two possible explanations:

1. To remember the miraculous *Ananei HaKavod*, the Clouds of Glory, which surrounded and protected us while traveling through the desert; or

---
1   The name the siddur uses to describe Pesach.
2   The name the siddur uses to describe Shavuos.
3   The name the siddur uses to describe Sukkos.
4   *Sukkah* 11b.

2. To remember the fact that while traveling through the desert, we camped in hut-like structures.

Whatever the case, neither of these reasons seem to suggest an element of *simchah* (happiness). Perhaps it would be most appropriate to refer to Sukkos as *z'man zichroneinu*, the time of our remembrance (i.e., the remembering of our desert travels).

Defining Happiness

It would be helpful to begin by first establishing some definitions. What is happiness?

Happiness is not a state of *having*. If this were so, happiness would be the result of what each of us was able to accumulate in our lives. Older and wealthier people would theoretically be happier than younger people (who generally have less) and those who are less fortunate. But we know that this is not always the case. Furthermore, happiness would forever be dependent on things outside of the self — externals that could cease after a time.

Happiness, as well, is much too important and central to life than simply being a state of *being*, either. A state of being focuses on life at a particular moment in the present: the here and now. However, not every moment in life is joyous, nor meant to be. People get sick, relationships shatter, individuals experience traumas and have to deal with the aftermath. King Solomon writes[5] that there is a special time for everything in life, and each emotion has its appropriate hour and place.

Happiness, therefore, must be a state of *becoming* — a process of becoming happier: happier than one is now.[6] When we think of happiness as a state of becoming, our lives become a process of continued growth and continuous effort in reaching a higher personal level than where we stand at the moment.

The holiest part of a *sukkah* is its roof, the *s'chach*,[7] which has to be

---

5 Ecclesiastes 3:1.
6 Tal Ben-Shahar, *Happier: Learn the Secrets to Daily Joy and Lasting Fulfillment* (New York: McGraw-Hill Education, 2007).
7 *S'chach* is compared to other holy articles, such as *tzitzis* or a *lulav*, which need to be discarded in

situated low enough over one's head that he can see it and constantly be mindful of it.[8] There is an interesting *halachah*, however, which states that for a *sukkah* to be kosher, its *s'chach* must provide more shade than sunlight.[9] In other words, the happiest holiday and the holiest aspect of that holiday center on the premise that there be more darkness than light — that G-d is to be found within the darkness, not the light. How can this be?

First and Second Light

Essentially, there are two types of light — first and second light:

- When G-d created the world, He created a light — the first light — that was so holy that humankind was unable to tolerate and live with it, so He hid and reserved it for *tzaddikim*, righteous individuals, yet to come.[10]

- The second light, created on the fourth day of Creation (along with the sun, the moon, and the stars), remains as people know it today. This light endures because it is a byproduct of that first holy light — a *result* of holiness.

Our Lights

Each of us experiences first and second "lights" in our lives. At times, we become consumed by particular experiences and invest all our energies therein. Perhaps we spend time in Eretz Yisrael, attend an inspiring lecture, or read a life-altering book, and become convinced that we can completely revamp our lives. The inspiration fills us and instills in us a desire for change and betterment; very often, we begin that journey of transformation. However, the first light cannot remain with us because it is too powerful, far beyond the scope of what the average human being can tolerate.

---

a dignified manner (see *Mishnah Berurah* 638:24).
8   *Sukkah* 2a.
9   *Orach Chaim* 631.
10 *Bereishis Rabbah* 3:6.

Life goes on and we become reacquainted with our old patterns. We no longer find ourselves in Eretz Yisrael, but rather immersed in our college studies; the lecture we just attended remains in our minds for a few days, maybe even weeks, but we find ourselves thrust back into our regular work routines; or we begin charting out a new life course for ourselves based on that uplifting book, but family matters force their way into our plans and life becomes hectic once again. In other words, the first light is incredibly powerful — but rarely lasts.

We experience the second light when we *reinvest* ourselves in that which we once experienced — when we take it upon ourselves to start learning Torah regularly once again in combination with our college schedule or when we decide to set a few moments aside from our busy work schedule to find some time for personal reflection. Second light means bringing ourselves to take small steps toward more meaning and fulfillment, instead of (temporarily, in most cases) changing the totality of our lives, all at once.

Second light lasts because of the efforts we invest once first light diminishes. Second light endures because we were given or took for ourselves a taste of first light and chose to hang onto a few of its rays.

In essence, first light is a gift from G-d — a glimpse of how awesome we can become; but second light allows each of us to bring some of that awesomeness into actuality — in a healthy way — without becoming wholly consumed.

Finding G-d within the Darkness

G-d is neither a part of the first or second light because He transcends both; G-d transcends all forms of finite definition. Defining G-d means turning an infinite being into something finite, turning a concept into a definition. G-d can be found within the darkness, within the *Ananei HaKavod*, because if He were to reveal His absolute clarity to our finite eye, we would not be able to tolerate the extent of His infiniteness. G-d is found within the darkness, in the shade of the *s'chach* (and within our challenges), because He does not belong in any finite box that any human being places Him. The comfort of the surrounding *Ananei HaKavod* during our forty-year journey through the desert (and the *sukkah* in which we presently dwell) was not that they directed us exactly where we needed to go and solved all of life's challenges as they arose, but rather that they acted as a guide — a sign from G-d, reassuring us that He knew the way and was leading us on the appropriate path. Even when we could not always sense His footprints walking alongside us in the sand, He was still there carrying us forward.

Happiness Is Not Knowing

Happiness is the state of becoming more than who we currently are. In other words, it means becoming more wholesome.

Happiness is not about knowing everything about every occurrence all of the time, but rather, knowing that each of us is placed in a particular situation because there is something that we have to offer it.

Happiness is not about blindly accepting pain and suffering, but about picking ourselves up again because we know that our time on earth is not yet over and that there is still something left for us to achieve.

Happiness as a state of becoming means realizing that we are part of something much larger than our own individual selves, and that we are each called upon to attach our individual fragments to that larger whole.

Collective Happiness

While Pesach celebrates collective freedom and Shavuos celebrates a collective covenant, Sukkos celebrates collective happiness. The Rabbis[11] teach that it would be fitting for the entire Jewish nation to build a *sukkah* large enough to include all of its members. How?

The idea is that, on Sukkos, the focus is not about the materialistic houses and objects that we amass in life. Those things highlight differences between people. Sukkos offers the opportunity for the greatest levels of unity, the most wholeness, because it is the time in which we focus on becoming — focusing on the root-soul that unites us, and understanding how each of us truly completes our nation's fragmented whole.

---

11 *Sukkah* 27b.

Sukkos cannot be referred to as *z'man zichroneinu* because remembering our past focuses on who we once were — not on who we are capable of becoming. Becoming whole within ourselves and at one with our people cannot be defined by materialistic and ego-differences of our pasts. Unity must be future-driven. It is about what we can accomplish tomorrow by working together today.

QUESTIONS FOR REFLECTION

- When have I experienced true joy or happiness? Who was a part of this?

- To whom in my life am I a source of joy or happiness?

4

TO KINDLE A FLAME BURIED WITHIN: CHANUKAH

A Seemingly Old Story

The story seems old. Standing up for their values and beliefs, a small group of Jews waged war against the mighty Greeks, who forbade them to live full Jewish lives. The Jews emerged victorious and reclaimed the Temple, only to find it in ruins and its oils desecrated. Miraculously, they found a small jug of oil still bearing the seal of the *Kohen Gadol*, the High Priest — enough to last but one day — and proceeded to kindle the Menorah, which astonishingly remained aflame for eight days.

In truth, the Greeks did not dislike Judaism as a whole (at least not at first). Greek culture and philosophy place great emphasis on aesthetic beauty and intellectual reasoning. In the eyes of the Greeks, the Beis HaMikdash, the Holy Temple, was a beautiful work of art and our Torah was a lofty philosophical work from which one could gain tremendous amounts of wisdom.[1] What really bothered the Greeks, however, were those aspects of Jewish life that superseded human comprehension. They initially forbade us from celebrating Shabbos, Rosh Chodesh (the new month), and *bris milah* (circumcision)[2] — *mitzvos* that specifically pertain to G-d's transcendence over human reason — in the hopes of ultimately destroying our connection to the Torah and G-dliness as a whole.[3]

---

1 This explains why the Torah was translated from Hebrew into Greek (*Megillah* 9a; Maharal, *Ner Mitzvah*).
2 *Megillas Antiochus* 1:11.
3 Rambam, *Hilchos Chanukah* 3:1; Maharal, *Ner Mitzvah*.

Chanukah's Uniqueness

As we have seen, each of our holidays centers on a unique miracle and particular theme. The question arises: should Chanukah's focus be on the miraculous war against the large Greek army and their Hellenistic ideology[4] or should its spotlight shine on the sacred oil that lasted for eight days when it only had the capacity to burn for one?[5]

Moreover, after we re-entered the Beis HaMikdash, why didn't we begin producing new oil from the onset? It was certainly permitted for us to do so. Why did we expend additional effort in searching for any remaining oil, specifically that bearing the seal of the *Kohen Gadol*?

Tamar's Loyalty

Parshas Vayeishev,[6] which contains in it the incident between Judah and Tamar, is always read near the holiday of Chanukah. It is a puzzling narrative: Tamar dresses as a harlot and has relations with her father-in-law, Judah. Prior to his departure, she requests that he leave his ring, garment, and staff with her as payment for their brief encounter. Three months pass and Judah is told that his daughter-in-law, Tamar, has become pregnant by means of harlotry. Ignorant to the fact that he is the cause for her pregnancy, Judah orders that she be taken outside and executed, at which point she reveals the ring, the garment, and the staff of the one with whom she had relations. Recognizing his own items, Judah realizes and admits that it was he who was responsible.[7]

There is a story told of Abraham the *Malach*, the son of Rabbi DovBer of Mezritch, the Maggid. One day, as a child, he came bursting into his father's study in tears. He explained to his father that while playing hide-and-seek with his friends, he had hidden himself so well that nobody was able to find him. When he came out of his hiding spot to reveal himself to his friends, he saw that they had all turned to playing other games and had given up trying to find him. He was crying because everyone had aban-

---

4   As read in *Al HaNissim*.
5   *Shabbos* 21b.
6   Genesis 37:1-40:23.
7   Ibid. 38:1-26.

doned hope of his returning, thinking that he had left forever.

In many ways, this story and the above narrative of Judah and Tamar depict the relationship we have with G-d. Shortly after their creation, the first human beings began playing hide-and-seek together with G-d in *Gan Eden*, the Garden of Eden. At first, Adam and Eve hid out of embarrassment about their nakedness and disobedience amidst the trees of the garden,[8] but then it became time for G-d to hide. Sadly, G-d hid Himself so well that, over the years, humanity began giving up hope of His existence and stopped looking for Him altogether.[9]

Each of us is created with a spark (or piece) of G-d buried within us.[10] True, we may not always behave perfectly, and indeed we may slip and make mistakes at times, but we never lose our deep connection to Him. Just as Judah suspected Tamar of engaging in immoral relations, so too are we suspected of betraying our relationship with our Husband. But no! We point to our *neshamos*, our souls, and cry out to Him: "We are still here! Yes, You may have hidden Yourself in the exile all of these years, but we have remained faithful!"[11]

The Flame Within

The Lubavitcher Rebbe articulates a fundamental tenet of Chassidic thought: that each Jew is a candle waiting to be kindled. He teaches[12] that the lump of wax represents our bodies while the wick represents our souls. Neither serve any function unless joined together toward the common purpose of creating a flame, thereby uniting both physical and metaphysical aspects of our beings. In truth, each of us has a small jug of oil buried deep within, still bearing the seal of the *Kohen Gadol* (more specifically, the seal of G-d). After the Greeks realized that Judaism could not exist alongside their Hellenistic lifestyle, they sought to destroy us. However, no matter how much they desecrated the Beis HaMikdash and massacred

---

8 Ibid. 3:8.
9 *Degel Mechaneh Ephraim, Parshas Tzav*.
10 Genesis 2:7; Tanya 2.
11 *Bas Ayin, Drush L'Chanukah, Parshas Vayeishev*.
12 Yehuda Avner, *The Prime Ministers: An Intimate Narrative of Israeli Leadership* (New Milford: Toby Press, 2010), 445–446.

and enslaved our people, they were never able to find that tiny jug — the pureness that only a divine being could plant deep within.[13]

Reb Shlomo Carlebach teaches[14] that there is the light of the sun and the moon that govern the parameters of time, but there is the light of a candle that transcends both. While each of the great luminaries weakens or grows larger as the days pass by, regardless of how much the flame of a candle shares its light with others, its worth never diminishes.

The Courage to Kindle Your Own Light

We can debate whether the miracle of Chanukah ought to center on the war between opposing Jewish and Hellenistic values or whether its focus ought to remain on the small jug of oil lasting longer than expected. Whatever the case, perhaps the greatest miracle is that we had the courage to set the oil aflame at the onset.

How many times do we have aspirations in life, but never act on them because we convince ourselves that we will ultimately fail? How many times do we give up on our dreams before even beginning to bring them to fruition?

One central lesson of Chanukah is that when all seems dark and lost, when our enemies (i.e., the anxiety we feel when confronted with uncertainty, fear, or doubt) attack our personal temple and desecrate our *Kodesh HaKodashim*, our Holy of Holies, we can stand up and dispel darkness with light.

For, no matter how bleak reality may seem — no matter how hopeless — darkness can never exist alongside light…even if it is but a small flame. Each of us, without exception, has that strength buried within ourselves to ignite that spark.

The Darkest Month

The holiday of Chanukah is celebrated during the month of Kislev, the darkest of Jewish months. We kindle our menorahs as if to shout out to

---

13 *Sefer HaMaamarim MiLikut*, Vol. 2 (Kislev-Shvat), *Parshas Mikeitz 5738/1977*.
14 Shlomo Katz, *The Soul of Chanukah: Teachings of Rabbi Shlomo Carlebach* (Mosaica Press, 2013), 46–47.

G-d, "We are still here! It is the darkest time of the year and we have not felt close to You since the holidays of Rosh Hashanah, Yom Kippur, and Sukkos during the month of Tishrei…but we are still here and still believe in the relationship between us!"

We kindle the Chanukah lights with pure oil, akin to that used in the Beis HaMikdash bearing the seal of the *Kohen Gadol*, as if to point to our soul and remind G-d of the pure piece of Himself that He left buried within us.[15]

A Shared, Unified Light

Each Shabbos, we kindle two candles to brighten up our homes. For eight days of the year, we tap into a unique, inner energy that empowers each of us to brighten the world around us.

Be the light you want to see in our seemingly dark world. Ignite your soul and inspire others to kindle theirs as well. Now is your time to shine. Do not pass up the opportunity because you feel another will shine brighter or burn longer than you — for you possess a light that is missing from the collective flame, waiting to be added to the fire of holiness…the torch of your people which has remained burning throughout the ages.

---

15 *Bas Ayin, Drush L'Chanukah, Parshas Vayeishev.*

QUESTIONS FOR REFLECTION

- When have I felt most lost in life? When have I doubted myself the most?

- Have I ever had aspirations that I wanted to fulfill but never took the steps to actualize them?

- What can I do in my life to allow more room for creative thinking and opportunities to dream?

5

ACTIVE CHOOSING: PURIM KATAN

What does it mean to choose?
To have the freedom to choose?

Who's in Charge?

There is a fundamental dilemma many of us grapple with on a daily basis:

- If G-d orchestrates the world, then His creations cannot have free will.

- If humankind has free will, G-d cannot wholly be in charge.

On the one hand, Judaism teaches[1] that G-d is the Ultimate Being: always existing[2] and never changing.[3] He was, is, and always will be.[4] He is the Supreme Creator, and because He created each of us, He knows infinitely more about us than we even know about ourselves.

Judaism also believes that G-d has a plan. That somehow, even when His presence cannot always be felt, G-d is still running the show.[5] Yet, G-d also calls on each of us to join in that plan — to be, as the Rabbis taught, His partners in completing the wonders of Creation.[6]

Judaism also explains that G-d does not remain stagnant.[7] While He

---
1 *Derech Hashem* 1.
2 Isaiah 43:13.
3 Malachi 3:6.
4 Isaiah 44:6; the *Adon Olam* prayer (found in most editions of the siddur).
5 Akin to the type of love between siblings (see chapter 8).
6 *Shabbos* 119b.
7 As seen in chapter 1.

is perfect and complete — and always has been — He constantly involves Himself in[8] and renews existence with each passing second.[9] From this perspective, created in His image and likeness, we too are not bound by the confines of stagnation. We can break free. We can choose to be different today from how we were yesterday, and different tomorrow from how we are today. Though G-d created linear time, He blessed each of us with the choice of how to use our time as we live out our lives.

False Security

The narrative of the Book of Esther is fraught with drama. Already in the third chapter, the wicked Haman proposes a decree — later sealed with the king's royal signet ring — to have all Jewish men, women, and children murdered.[10]

When Mordecai, the archetypic *tzaddik* (righteous individual), learns about the decree, he sits in the king's palace-courtyard mourning for the future.[11] When the Jews in each of the 127 provinces receive news of the decree, there is great turmoil. They too tear their clothing and sit in mourning.[12]

Safe within the confines of the king's palace, however, Esther — her Jewishness unbeknown — finds it too unbearable to see her uncle in such anguish. Ironically, she is oblivious to any decree issued against her people. She learns of Haman's evil plan, but protests her ability to affect change. Esther correctly knows that no person is able to enter the king's inner-chamber without permission; approaching the king to plead for mercy without being invited would be akin to committing suicide![13] She refuses to take action and initially denies Mordecai's request that she approach the king on behalf of her people.

---

8   *Derech Hashem* 2:1.
9   *Kedushas Levi, Parshas Bereishis*.
10 Esther 3:8-11.
11 Ibid. 4:1.
12 Ibid. 4:3.
13 Ibid. 4:11.

To Act or Not to Act

Then come Mordecai's fateful words: "Don't imagine that you alone, out of all the Jews, will escape by being in the king's palace. If you remain quiet now, *the Jews will find relief and safety through a different route*, while you and your father's household will be destroyed! And who knows — perhaps the monarchy came your way precisely for this moment?"[14]

Esther is faced with a choice: to act or not to act. Should she reveal her true self or remain hidden? At present, she is safe within the confines of the king's palace, out of harm's reach and unbeknown to anyone as a Jew. However, this is not who she is. This is not who she was meant to be. This is not all that she *can* be.

True, G-d directs the show. Still, His name is not mentioned even once within the narrative of the Book of Esther, because perhaps one of the underlying messages of the Purim story is that G-d wants *us* to choose. He wants us to be active partners, not passive receivers. Life is meant to be lived, not received. Unlike Adam and Eve in the opening chapter of the Book of Genesis, who passively receive from G-d, we are commanded to work the land — and to a larger extent, all of physicality.[15] Free will means that, despite G-d's master-plan, each of us has the opportunity to actively choose to involve ourselves therein, as opposed to letting it unfold in front of our eyes and abandoning our involvement altogether.

The Paradox of Happiness

The Rabbis teach[16] that just as when the month of Av enters, we are to decrease our *simchah*, our joy, so too when we enter the month of Adar, are we to increase our *simchah*. The Halachah lists several activities we are to refrain from during the month of Av (eating meat, purchasing new clothes, bathing for pleasure, etc.) — as a way of further decreasing our enjoyment.[17]

Why? There is a general principle in Halachah that if a ruling is pre-

---

14 Ibid. 4:13.
15 Genesis 2:15.
16 *Taanis* 29a.
17 *Orach Chaim* 550 and onwards.

scribed in one situation, it can oftentimes be applied in an almost identical situation (as in the case of Pesach and Sukkos, which both occur on the 15th of their respective months).[18] If the Rabbis teach that we ought to increase our *simchah* during the month of Adar *because* we decrease it during the month of Av, then perhaps we ought to adhere to a list of activities to partake in to *increase* our joy, as well?!

In truth, it is easy to feel sadness. It is easy to find fault with the world and the people around us. And it is easy to convince others to see the negative around them as well.

It is more difficult to feel happiness. Joy takes persistent effort. It is an active choice. Sadness is easier because it remains passive. All we need to do is take a moment to look at the world around us and we can be sure to find no lack of poverty, sickness, divorce, or abuse therein.

Being in a state of *simchah* does not mean that we should ignore these difficult realities, but rather that we should not dwell on them and allow them to overcome and overpower us. We must assess, accept, and transform the situations in which we find ourselves, and not deny or pretend to live within a different reality.

This is why the Halachah places limits on our sadness by providing us with a list of activities to refrain from. If kept within limits, sadness can be a meaningful element in life because it allows individuals to grow and learn from their sorrowful experiences. But it is only positive if it is a means to an end — if it is constructive. If sadness is let loose and left unchecked — an open-ended prescription to an emotion without any specified dosage — it can be disastrous to each of us and society at large.

Happiness, by contrast, is personal. It has the potential to be lasting, because it is something that we each choose, as opposed to something that chooses us. When the month of Adar enters, we increase our *simchah*, and we do not require any lists or recipes for how to do it. Real joy is internal, not dependent on other people or events. But for it to be real, it has to be ours: belonging to, and cultivated by, each of us.

---

18   Pesach begins on the 15th of Nisan, Sukkos begins on the 15th of Tishrei.

Rare, but Precious Opportunities

Purim Katan lasts but one day. It occurs seven times in a nineteen-year cycle — in each Jewish "leap-year" — and has no real *halachic* significance other than the fact that it is a remembrance that the actual holiday of Purim would normally be celebrated on that day, if not for the leap year. Still, we acknowledge it nonetheless. We could passively ignore it, as Esther could have done within the safety and shelter of the king's palace — but we do not.

Life is a choice between active and passive living. Both are possible. Still, G-d did not create us to merely achieve — He created each of us to excel: to step beyond the social norm, beyond what others expect of us! Why should we exert ourselves when life will ultimately run its course and if G-d has already set His script in motion? Because we each have the capability to; this is our calling.

Ultimately, G-d will redeem His people whether we act or not. However, each choice we make (whether conscious or not) has a great effect on who we are (and are capable of becoming) on a micro-level and the collective people of which we are a part on a macro-level. In the ultimate future, G-d will bring true *simchah* to all of us. By choosing joy now, we can internalize, experience, and live it.

QUESTIONS FOR REFLECTION

- Who do I feel is in control of my life?

- Am I more inclined to notice the positive aspects in my life or more prone to focus on the negative ones?

- How many times throughout my day do I make active choices? How often do I let others make choices for me?

6

POTENTIAL ACTUALIZED: PURIM

Life in Three Stages

Life can be divided into three stages: conception, reality, and post-reality (life after death):

1. During the period of conception, we exist within the confines of our mother's womb, engrossed in physicality. All that is expected of us at this point in life is to grow and develop. We are given all our organs, but they are nonfunctioning; we have eyes, ears, arms, and legs, but none of these can express themselves or offer us any real benefit. We each must eventually take leave of this stage in life, from the shelter of the womb.

2. Next, we enter the second stage of life. We are suddenly "reborn," but into a different kind of life. In this new life, we are able to use our senses. Relying on the potentials nurtured within the womb, we can now begin using our eyes to see and our noses to smell, and we become fascinated by the many wonders amidst the physical world in which we now find ourselves. This new life is still very much like the first, still physical, but it offers us opportunities to generate meaning from our existence.

3. Eventually, (now as adults) we approach the third and final stage: life after physical life. During physical life, we use our bodies to actualize the potentials given us while inhabiting our initial womb (inside our mothers). By cultivating a meaningful life outside of that shelter, we

prepare ourselves, yet again, to face another form of birth — to stand before and greet our Maker.[1]

A Textual Nuance

The Talmud[2] points out a subtle nuance within the text of the Book of Esther. About to enter the king's inner chamber to plead on behalf of her people, the text reads, "After the third day, Esther dressed herself in *malchus* (in royalty) and stood in the courtyard of the king's living quarters..."[3]

For the sentence's grammar to be correct, however, it should have included the noun, *bigdei malchus* (clothing of royalty), instead of only the adjective, *malchus*. The Talmud explains that the text omits the word "clothing" in order to teach readers that Esther's dressing up in royalty means that she was clothed in *ruach hakodesh*, in prophecy. The courtyard in which she stood is referred to by the Talmud[4] as *Beis HaTzelamim*, the Hall of Carved Statues, because its walls were lined with images and statues of Persian deities. It was there that Esther lost her connection to prophecy.

Esther, representing the archetypal soul trapped within the human body, is forced to pass through the corridor of physicality (represented by the Persian statues) on her way to greet the king — but she freezes. She encounters a physicality that is so daunting that she loses faith in herself.

Each of the statues represent a different aspect of her being that screams out to her that she will fail.[5] She *stands* — she doesn't fully walk through the passageway, as the text should have read — because Esther feels restricted from developing into the individual she knows (deep down) she is capable of becoming. She settles for a life of physicality, a life within the second womb, and not her ultimate potential of eventually transcending and standing before her Father in Heaven.

However, the narrative does not end there. Esther regains her com-

---

1 Aryeh Kaplan, *Encounters* (Jerusalem: Moznaim Publishing Corporation, 1990), 19–21.
2 *Megillah* 14b.
3 Esther 5:1.
4 *Megillah* 15b.
5 Avraham Sutton, *Purim Light* (Jerusalem: Targum Press, 2010), 22.

posure. She looks, not at the fragments of herself that weigh her down (the heavy statues), but at the pieces of herself — each strength that she possesses — that she can glue together. She looks, not at who she is at that moment, but at the person she is capable of becoming at a later time. As soon as she reconnects with her Source, her true self (her soul), the King admits her into His inner chamber — into His *Kodesh HaKodashim*, His Holy of Holies.[6]

This seemingly minor textual detail encompasses the essence of what the holiday of Purim represents. Purim mirrors the middle stage of life, the years in which we articulate our souls within our bodies as we prepare to ultimately transcend.

Trilogy of Redemption

This three-stage journey of life follows the process of *geulah*, redemption, observed in the late winter holiday trilogy of Tu b'Shevat, Purim, and Pesach:

- Tu b'Shevat, the New Year of the trees, begins this process. It occurs on the 15th of Shevat, just 30 days prior to Purim (or more specifically, *Shushan Purim*) and 60 days prior to Pesach. The significance lies in the fact that each of these holidays centers on the moon — specifically a full moon, which symbolizes a maximum capacity for growth. The Rabbis teach[7] that one who is wise is one who is able to see the birth of something, *nolad*, which bears the same Hebrew root as the word *molad*, the new moon. Wisdom means being able to envision the beginning of something and what might transpire therefrom: the potential budding within its conception. On the day following Tu b'Shevat, to the external, human eye, a tree looks exactly the same as it did the previous day; it cannot see that the sap has already begun rising inside.[8] Likewise, the inner dimensions of each of us — our souls — cannot be viewed through the lens of physicality; externally,

---

6   Esther 5:2; ibid.
7   *Tamid* 32a.
8   Avraham Arieh Trugman, *Seeds and Sparks* (Jerusalem: Targum Press, 2003), 143.

it is difficult to detect the tremendous holiness buried within a person when we find ourselves continuously distracted by the transgressions we think he commits.

- Toward the end of a long winter, Tu b'Shevat celebrates the genesis of potential. Purim represents the point where we begin actualizing our potentials. It is the middle stage of the lifespan in which we look deep within ourselves and begin responding to our unique callings and directing our lives toward becoming the people we know ourselves capable of becoming.

- Subsequently, Pesach represents the journey of life after physical life, the final stage. It is the time of feeling complete redemption and closeness to G-d following the miraculous Exodus from Egypt and the splitting of the Sea of Reeds. With the constant, overflowing, and very open miracles that we commemorate, it is almost impossible to not experience feelings of spiritual transcendence.

Bipolar Perspectives of Creation

The Torah includes two readings of the Creation narrative,[9] as if to suggest that it can be read from two opposing perspectives:

1. In the first instance, G-d creates everything. Creation is an *isarusa d'l'eila*, an arousal from Above to below in which reality passively receives divine blessings — akin to an infant resting peacefully within his mother's womb and passively receiving nourishment from her.

2. In the second, however, G-d recedes and waits for His creations to initiate a relationship; it centers on an *isarusa d'l'sata*, an arousal from below – where there is "no individual to work the land"[10] — to Above. From the second perspective, G-d gave Creation potential, but it is up to each of us to actualize that potential by cultivating the land (physicality) to bring G-d's potential into actuality.

---
9 Genesis 1–2.
10 Ibid. 2:5.

Focusing on What Lies Beneath

At first glance, the Book of Esther seems devoid of any *siyata di'Shemaya*, Divine intervention, just as the sap's development within the trees appears nonexistent immediately following Tu b'Shevat. Each of our potentials are only possible to reach if we focus on what lies beneath the physical casing of our souls (our bodies), just as G-d can be seen in the Purim narrative only if we choose to look beyond the surface of its seemingly random series of events. Purim is the time for each of us to take part in, and take ownership of our lives: never settling for that which lies above the surface — reality as we perceive it — but probing the limits others have envisioned for us and tapping into the parts of ourselves we never knew achievable.

QUESTIONS FOR REFLECTION

- Do I feel that I have nurtured and articulated the potentials given to me within the womb? If not, which could I focus on that would allow for further development?

- Which potentials do I wish I could have nurtured within my own children during pregnancy? If I were to have more children, which potentials would I hope to impart to them prior to birth?

7

THE JOURNEY: FROM PURIM TO PESACH

The Power of Fifteen

There are two holidays that fall on the 15th of the month: Pesach[1] and Sukkos.[2] It is somewhat easy to understand why these holidays occur when they do, based on the uniqueness of the number 15. From the onset, 15 shares the same Hebrew numerical value as one of G-d's names, י-ה. Secondly, the 15th of any month is the day in which the moon reaches its fullest shape; just as the moon constantly develops until then, so too must we constantly be growing and reaching greater capacities in that which we set out to achieve. The waxing and waning of the moon symbolizes the pattern of *galus* and *geulah*, exile and redemption, as well: just when it seems as though G-d has forgotten about us, we experience yet another rebirth.

Purim, however, is celebrated on the 14th of Adar, because fourteen is a number that represents transcendence. Fourteen in Hebrew has the numerical value of the word *yad* (hand), and appears numerous times throughout the Torah. During the Exodus narrative, for instance, the Torah describes how G-d redeemed us from Egyptian bondage with a *yad chazakah* (a strong hand).[3] During the miraculous splitting of the Sea of Reeds, by contrast, we stood witness to G-d's *yad hagedolah* (His great hand).[4]

---

1 The 15th of Nisan.
2 The 15th of Tishrei.
3 Exodus 13:9.
4 Ibid. 13:9; 14:31.

What is the difference between these two types of hands?

- G-d's *yad chazakah* symbolizes His strength and sovereignty within the laws of nature. The laws of nature are set and unchangeable, just as G-d has an aspect of Himself which is firm and dominating (manifested by the name *Elokim*).

- G-d's *yad hagedolah*, however, represents His ability to transcend the laws of nature (inferred by His name *Havaya*).[5]

Logic vs. Transcendence

The Sea of Reeds posed a direct threat to our future existence as a nation. The powerful Egyptian army was closing in on us, while all that lay ahead of us was the sea. Moses raised his hands to G-d, but was told, perhaps ironically, *not* to pray, but to walk forth through the sea.

Moses is always associated with the trait of *chochmah*, wisdom. After all, it is he who brought the Torah down from Mount Sinai and he who taught us its *mitzvos*. For the rational mind, it would seem illogical to progress forward through the water; clearly we would die once the waters covered our heads.

Who would be the first to enter the waters?

- The tribe of Reuben (connoting "seeing") was unable to move forward because its dominant trait was not believing in something until only after it had personally seen it. Its members could not accept the notion that G-d would split the sea until actually witnessing its occurrence.

- Likewise, the tribe of Simon (connoting "hearing") would not step foot into the sea because its dominant trait was only acting on an idea after first hearing a safe and promising report of its success from another.

---

5   An individual's right hand is usually his primary (or great) hand. In Kabbalah, the right side of an entity is always linked with *chesed*, loving-kindness, which has the ability to soften the rigidity of *gevurah* (associated with the left side).

- In similar vein, the tribe of Levi (implying "goodness"[6]) would not advance into the sea because the dominant trait of its members was to only better themselves after G-d first bestowed His goodness on them.

Nahshon ben Aminadab, however, from the tribe of Judah (meaning, "praise"), was the only one capable of jumping into the sea.[7] He represented those of us who admit that we may not understand every detail of G-d's mastery over the natural world, but nonetheless, we acknowledge His superiority and His ability to intervene therein.

It is easy to connect to G-d within the domain of the natural world. Many people experience deep feelings of serenity or spiritual awakenings while spending time alone in nature. Seeking G-d in the realm of *Havaya*,[8] however, requires people to praise and acknowledge Him even when He may not always be seen (Reuben), be proven by others (Simon), or during times when He does not appear to be bestowing goodness on us (Levi). On the level of *Havaya*, only G-dliness exists;[9] logic and illogic, good and evil are all equal manifestations of Him.

Beyond Logic

Within the Persian Empire,[10] the wicked Haman strove to murder each Jewish man, woman, and child. His anger was aroused when Mordecai refused to bow down to him. According to the rational mind, bowing down and discarding the Torah seems logical. Up until this point, the Torah had been forced upon us many years prior at Mount Sinai, so to speak.[11] Purim is the celebration of our re-acceptance of the Torah and re-affirmation of

---

6   Leah assigned the name Levi because she hoped that after having three sons, Jacob would feel more attached to her (Genesis 29:34).
7   *Mechilta* 14:22.
8   It is easier to sense G-d's presence when He performs open miracles within the natural world that we can witness, in contrast to feeling His presence when it manifests itself in ways transcendent to the natural world that we cannot always sense.
9   *Ein od milvado*, there is none other than Him (Deuteronomy 4:35).
10 Approximately 357 BCE.
11 *Shabbos* 88a.

our relationship with G-d[12] — transcending the rationale which should have dictated that we abandon our relationship and not put ourselves at risk of annihilation.

The Rabbis teach[13] that we should begin preparing for a *Yom Tov* 30 days prior to its arrival. Since Purim occurs exactly 30 days before Pesach, we can infer that Purim is, in fact, the beginning of our Pesach preparations. How does Purim, the 14th of Adar, prepare us for Pesach, the 15th of Nisan? While it makes sense to redeem us on the 15th of the month because of its association with G-d's name, G-d still liberated us with a *yad chazakah*, with a firmness that was embodied by the laws of nature (to an extent).[14] The entire purpose of our redemption from Egypt was ultimately to receive the gift of the Torah on Mount Sinai[15] — an event which was only possible if we each transcended our minor differences and united with our brethren as one nation with one heart.[16]

Applying the logic of those faced with the daunting task of crossing the sea despite no logical method, it is an impossible feat that we could overcome our differences and unite as a people with a shared vision if we only adhere to the labels we assign to ourselves, the labels *we* believe to be most logical. Logic looks to the Creation narrative and reads, "And G-d created humankind in His image..."[17] Thus, since one's likeness is different from another's, he must be more G-dly than the other and subsequently superior. However, the verse does not end there: "...male *and* female He created them."[18] G-d has no human form, yet each of us are created within the image of our Maker, because His image is comprised of opposites (male and female). Wisdom *should* dictate that since each of us possesses some

---

12 Ibid.
13 *Pesachim* 6a.
14 Although the many open miracles of the Exodus were indeed manipulations of the natural order (such as the Ten Plagues and the Splitting of the Reed Sea), Pesach is still only a preparation for the ultimate celebration of the receiving of the Torah yet to come. As transcendent as Pesach was (and is), it was only a stepping stone for an even greater level of revelation and outpouring of love that we collectively experienced on Shavuos.
15 Exodus 5:1.
16 Rashi, ibid. 19:2.
17 Genesis 1:27.
18 Ibid.

aspect of G-dliness that another lacks, we each are therefore incomplete until we unite with our brethren who appear different than us.

Seedlings of Potential

This is the correlation (and the journey) between Purim and Pesach. Although we are each given the potential to transcend our personal limitations on Purim, we will never be able to experience *geulah*, redemption, on Pesach until we first learn how to discard our external labels and come together as a united people. The *Yom Tov* of the 14th of Adar, Purim, *must* precede that of the 15th of Nisan, Pesach. The *geulah* began long ago when we first took leave from our Egyptian oppressors, but it is up to each of us to contribute our share in completing it in the present. The 30 days between Purim and Pesach are a journey of preparation. In order to reach it together, we must first come together.

QUESTIONS FOR REFLECTION

- Do I feel more comfortable around those whom I believe to be like me?

- Do my Pesach preparations consist only of ridding my home of *chametz* and making sure that everything (and everyone in my family) looks clean?

8

THE POTENTIAL TO LOVE: PESACH

The Two Faces of Creation

As we have seen in previous chapters, there are two ways to look at the Creation narrative:[1] G-d as above or G-d as within.

In the first instance, in the Creation described in the first chapter of the Book of Genesis, G-d appears above everything in existence — dominating all that He created. He is a hierarchy Being, the ultimate Being. G-d is the sole Creator Who creates within a series of commands ("G-d said, 'Let there be…' and there was…"). He sets rules for mankind and bestows upon them the mission of dominating over the animal and plant kingdoms; He charges humanity with the task of populating the earth and ensuring the survival of the human species.[2] Adam and the woman marry, but seemingly out of duty; their intent is not to grow together as a couple, but to ensure that a future generation will be born[3] — this is evident in the fact that the woman is not even given a name until the second chapter in the Book of Genesis.[4]

In the second perspective, in the second chapter of the Book of Genesis, however, Adam finds himself alone. He understands that he comes from dust of the earth[5] and to dust he shall eventually return.[6] Whereby in the beginning, Adam of the first chapter is a dignified being placed above

---

1 Genesis 1–2.
2 Ibid. 1:28.
3 Joseph B. Soloveitchik, *The Lonely Man of Faith* (New York: Doubleday Books, 1965).
4 Genesis 2:23.
5 Ibid. 2:27.
6 Ibid. 3:19.

all other creations, Adam of the second chapter is humble. He realizes that there is more to existence than replenishing a population, and he longs for a union that transcends the laws of nature; he desires a soul mate with whom he can enter a sacred relationship.[7]

Elokim and Havaya

G-d, too, expresses Himself within these two frames of reference:

1. *Elokim*, the G-d of nature,[8] creates within the laws of nature. He abides by His own rules and operates on the basis of reward and punishment after judging accurately. G-d as *Elokim* is a being detached from His creations, Who oversees reality but does not necessarily involve Himself in it on an intimate level. He instills a sense of awe in his creations, but not necessarily feelings of love. *Elokim* created time and space, and He chooses to act in accordance with the laws He created that govern time and space. Acting as *Elokim*, manifesting and expressing Himself solely through accurate and strict judgments, G-d could not have redeemed us from our Egyptian oppressors.

2. There is also, however, the aspect of G-d that is transcendent of the linear mentality inherit to Adam the First. In the case of Adam in the second chapter, G-d reveals Himself as a loving father. True, He remains alone, just as Adam the Second finds himself alone, but G-d as a loving father longs for a relationship with His creations rooted in love; He desires a partnership in which they continue completing His works of Creation.[9] This is the aspect of G-d revealed by the name *Havaya* and is rooted in *chesed*, unconditional love; only by manifesting Himself as *Havaya* was G-d able to transcend the rigid limits of reward and punishment and redeem us from slavery.

---

7   Soloveitchik, *The Lonely Man of Faith*.
8   The Sages note that the words *Elokim* and *hateva* ("nature") share the same Hebrew numeric value.
9   *Shabbos* 119b.

What Is Love?

G-d certainly loves us – to no end. But what is the definition of love? On our finite level, what enables us to transcend limitations and rigidity inherent to the mentality of Adam the First — essentially breaking free — and transition from the distant *Elokim* to the imminent *Havaya*?

Chassidic thought[10] teaches that there are two forms of love: love like fire and love like water. Both are radically different:

- Fire exists in a constant state of change. It begins small and the more one adds to it, the stronger, warmer, and more passionate it becomes. But a fire can burn out if not continuously refueled or it can lead to destruction if not carefully tamed.

- Water, by contrast, remains still and calm, only changing when external force is applied; water is oftentimes cool unless heat is generated from a secondary source.

Where fire represents a passionate love generated between husband and wife within marriage, love like water depicts the relationship between siblings. Marriage (and any relationship, for that matter) takes effort. Each spouse must constantly be on guard against how he or she acts, what is said, or which behaviors need to be avoided to strengthen that relationship. Fire is generated by combining two (or more) different substances — a fire-source and a substance to set aflame — just as marriage results from two individuals uniting to ignite a spark of shared interests and values. The potential is enormous, but if not properly nurtured and tamed, a marriage will ultimately fail.

Love between siblings, on the other hand, is continuously present, even when each one does not employ active efforts to maintain that relationship. It is the type of relationship that exists even when it is not felt — akin to the stillness of water when compared to the heat of dancing fire.

---

10 Sholom DovBer Schneerson, *Kuntreis Eitz Chaim* 2; *Kuntreis HaAvodah* 4.

Two Functions of the Human Heart

The human heart is comprised of two sides: the right sends blood to collect oxygen from the lungs and the left receives and distributes the newly oxygenated blood throughout the body. In Chassidic thought,[11] the receiving side represents physicality; it is the aspect of an individual known as the *nefesh habehamis*, the animal soul, that strives to direct a person toward mundane pursuits. This side, no less important to the full functioning of the heart, experiences emotions, but those emotions lack intellectual reason. They are desires not concerned with an outcome, but with immediate satisfaction. The side of physicality causes the individual to focus on himself and how he can advance his own well-being.

Like Adam the First, whose primary goal is to advance his own well-being, the left side prompts a person to place his own interests above those of others (hierarchy). Yes, he is likely to marry and perhaps even contribute to society in some or many ways, but only because he feels that he can gain thereby. The receiving side of our hearts leads us to seek passion, but this passion lacks the intellectuality that enables us to use it in meaningful and lasting ways. Should our hearts fail (G-d forbid!) — focusing only on themselves, the blood, and not on transporting oxygen to the brain — we too will ultimately expire.

The right side of our hearts, however, houses the *nefesh Elokis*, the G-dly soul, and directs us toward pursuing meaning. It receives guidance from the brain because it understands that emotions unaccompanied by intellect are like wild children without direction.

Fire or Water?

This passionate love like fire between us and G-d is short-lived, and if maintained at all, is only achieved by a select few *tzaddikim*, righteous individuals. It is a love like flaming coals,[12] and the closer we get to its heat, the more passion we add, in reality, the more distant we feel from the source — because no matter how heated a fire becomes, no matter how intense its flames roar, it will always want more fuel. A flame forever desires to rise

---
11 Tanya 9.
12 Ibid.

higher and is never content with the love it has been given. A love like fire is nearly impossible to maintain while living a life amidst the finite world.[13]

A love like water, by contrast, becomes a part of each of us to the extent that it calms us. Whereby a love like flaming coals is intense for a particular moment, its intensity will ultimately cease if not internalized and its passions used for higher, intellectual, and more sanctified purposes.[14] Love like water may remain virtually stagnant. It can even appear as though it doesn't exist, but we each know that it is always present. This is why, when Abraham and Sarah flee to Egypt, he requests that she notify the Egyptian ministers that she is his sister — and not his wife.[15] He fears his life will be cut short, because he knows that without her, he will remain incomplete. Abraham understands that he and Sarah are about to approach unknown, dangerous territory — an environment that will put their marriage at risk; he tells her that he wants to take their love of flaming coals and elevate it to a status of a love like water. Abraham desires to reach the point where no matter what obstacle he and Sarah encounter together, their love will remain calm and everlasting.

On Shavuos, we celebrate the wedding anniversary of our entering into a sacred covenant with our Spouse. Pesach thus symbolizes the weeks leading up to that awesome wedding day, which are filled with excitement and infatuation. On Pesach, it is hard not to experience a love of flaming coals. The totality of the *Yom Tov* is a re-enactment of the nonstop, open miracles that G-d performed for us in Egypt. Just as a *chassan* and *kallah*, a groom and bride, focus on nothing other than each other and their wedding, so too do we become infatuated with desires of uniting with our Beloved[16] — to the point that we interrupt our Seder just before eating the main meal to passionately sing *Hallel*: a spontaneous collection of praise, not resulting from a thought-out analysis of G-d's goodness to us, but out of pure joy that generates only from the emotional part of our hearts.[17]

---

[13] Tanya 50.
[14] Ibid. 44.
[15] *Bereishis* 12:13.
[16] A quick reading of King Solomon's Song of Songs (which is read on the Shabbos of Pesach) clearly demonstrates this love relationship.
[17] The reason why no blessing is recited prior to singing *Hallel* (Hai Gaon, as cited by many).

Potential for a Lasting Relationship

As quickly as Pesach comes and passes, and we breeze through the forty-nine days leading up to Shavuos, we soon find ourselves thrust back into mundane life — life prior to the spiritual arousal and fiery love that is generated in the initial stages of a relationship, but often diminishes as time passes. The mission becomes transforming our newly generated love of flaming coals into a lasting love like water. It is the task, as was with Abraham, of telling our Spouse that when the going gets tough, we long to remain forever in a relationship — akin to that of siblings, which is always present even when not strongly felt. We tell G-d that once the fanfare of the holiday recedes and we find ourselves forced back into a life of *galus*, exile, in which He no longer seems to perform open miracles for us, we still wish to maintain a closeness with Him. And, perhaps, if we experience Pesach authentically — each according to our own, unique relationship with our Maker — we will merit to pocket a few of these flaming coals, to take out and admire on occasion throughout the year and glean inspiration from them. Pesach generates the potential to love: love of ourselves and love of others.

QUESTIONS FOR REFLECTION

- With whom do I feel a love-like-fire (and love-like-water) relationship?

- What do I do to increase and strengthen my relationships with others? How can they be made stronger?

- What holds me back from forming (or strengthening) a relationship with someone?

9

BECOMING WHOLE AGAIN: SHAVUOS

From Singularity to Duality

Prior to Creation, G-d was the only existence. Shattering Himself, singularity became duality. A finite universe was born, but it was charged with the mission of ultimately becoming whole again.[1]

How does singularity become duality and vice versa? The Sages teach that G-d created us because He had a desire to engage in a relationship with another, and not just remain in a dwelling place amidst the upper worlds as an authoritarian figure.[2] For finite creations to exist alongside an infinite being, however, G-d had to "contract" himself and make space within Himself for them to dwell;[3] He "divided Himself," so to speak, allowing these shattered parts of Himself to scatter throughout the physical world and within each of His creations. To become whole again, we must find these pieces — seeing the G-dliness amidst the seemingly mundane — and elevate and unite them. Becoming whole again means that we are each incomplete on our own. Becoming one means uniting in holy matrimony with another on a journey of love. This is what transpires on Shavuos, and more specifically, the forty-nine day period between our engagement to G-d on Pesach and subsequent wedding on Shavuos.

---

1 Whole in the sense that the shattered fragments of G-dliness embedded within finite reality become re-united.
2 *Tanchuma, Naso* 7:1; *Shabbos* 119b.
3 Tanya 21, 48–49; *Kedushas Levi, Parshas Bereishis*.

The Creation of Man and Woman

G-d formed humankind on the sixth day of Creation as one hermaphroditic[4] being. He put the human into a deep sleep, separating the unified being and creating woman as a distinct entity from man.[5] Shortly after their separation, however, G-d instructed the man and woman not to remain content as two unique selves, but rather to strive for oneness again.[6]

If the purpose in creating man and woman was that they should be a unified whole, why initially separate them? Would it not have been more efficient for G-d to allow them to live as one being?

The journey of oneness mentioned above is, in fact, the essence of Judaism's understanding of marriage: G-d takes a soul and separates it into two so that it can learn how to become one again within the physical world through its own efforts.

Reconnecting through Time, Space, and Soul

This reconnecting of halves does not occur all at once, but gradually over time. Just as all of reality exists within one of three frames of reference — space, time, and soul (*olam*, *shanah*, and *nefesh*)[7] — so too do husband and wife unify in progression from frame to frame.[8] In the reality of space, male and female approach the union from different life experiences and environmental influences. They begin merging and learning how to occupy the same mental space. They start approaching life, not as two distant voices, but as one: by actualizing their inner oneness. As they become further entwined and advance into the framework of time, husband and wife develop a desire to spend each moment of life together; both cannot imagine experiencing holidays and lifecycle events without the other. Finally, entering the realm of soul, both individuals return to the state of complete oneness that they initially experienced prior to sep-

---

4 A creation (or human being) with both male and female features (*Bereishis Rabbah* 8:1).
5 Genesis 2:21.
6 Ibid. 2:24.
7 Rabbeinu Bechaya, Genesis 1:12.
8 Yitzchak Ginsburgh, *The Mystery of Marriage: How to Find True Love and Happiness in Married Life* (Jerusalem: Gal Einai Institute, 1999), 170–173.

aration; they do not experience or express emotions *toward* one another, but they *become* one another and live as one being.

Prerequisite for Achieving Unity

Just as man and woman unite in oneness through their relationship and not religion (connection and not authority),[9] so too can we. True unity is only possible if it is initiated on the level of relationship — the level of *ahavah*, love — where none of us is more superior or inferior to our fellow. Unity means looking not at our bodies — the physical aspects that make us different — but rather at our *neshamos*, our souls, buried within: the pieces of G-d embedded deeply within our very essences. Just as marriage follows the one-to-two-to-one pattern, so too must Jewish unity.

Reb Shlomo Carlebach touches on these two ideas in a teaching from *Parshas Vayeitzei*.[10] Rachel, Jacob's more beloved wife, represents *alma d'isgalya*, revealed beauty, while Leah symbolizes *alma d'iskasya*, concealed beauty. Rachel's beauty was evident from the moment one gazed upon her. One only came to notice the beauty of Leah, by contrast, after looking longer and more closely. The Sages teach that all G-d does is ultimately for the benefit of His creations;[11] every facet of reality is somehow a gift that can aid us in further actualizing aspects of our potentials. Similar to Rachel and Leah, however, some gifts take the form of revealed goodness while others remain concealed and only become realized in hindsight (if at all).

Seeing Beneath the Surface

By marrying Rachel at night — symbolizing a period of darkness and

---

9   Religion consists of a hierarchical system in which a superior being dictates a series of rules and commands to those who believe in and accept this authority. Relationships, by contrast, consist of mutual partnerships in which individuals come together, not out of fear of punishment or to advance their own well-being, but because they feel a strong connection.
10 Shlomo Katz, ed., *The Torah Commentary of Rabbi Shlomo Carlebach: Genesis, Part II* (Jerusalem: Urim Publications, 2013), 41–43.
11 A concept embodied by the Sage, Nachum Ish Gamzu, who would constantly comment, "*Gam zu l'tovah* — This too is for the best," regarding any apparent misfortune.

exile — Jacob was able to see the light of *geulah*, redemption, shimmering and waiting to be ignited (beauty amidst the darkness). Jacob, however, also marries Leah; he finds G-dliness in a place he never dreamed of. By marrying Leah, Jacob experiences beauty within another Jew whom he initially thought was nothing special. While Rachel gave lineage to the Mashiach ben Yosef, the initial Messiah who will generate the sparks of immediate redemption, Leah gives lineage to the Mashiach ben David, the one who will ultimately initiate the complete and final *geulah*.

In truth, both are needed. We must realize the beauty and passionate love in our lives, but also the underlying goodness that we may initially only glance at or deem unworthy. It is easy to build relationships with those with whom we feel an immediate attraction. The true yardstick for determining whether we have achieved unity, however, lies in our ability to create relationships with those with whom we may not initially feel drawn toward.

The Mashiach ben Yosef is important because, throughout life, we each experience moments of personal redemption and flashes of inspiration propelling us to growth. Still, personal redemptions are not enough if they are not shared with others, if others are not included in a collective *geulah*. The Mashiach ben David paves the path to complete *geulah* because he embodies the notion that a spark of G-d lies within the other, whom we perceive to be different. To achieve wholeness, we must ignite that spark within ourselves and collectively illuminate the world around us by collecting and connecting our many flames.

Whereby Pesach is an immediate, personal *geulah* from our burdensome Egyptian suffering — Mashiach ben Yosef, Shavuos symbolizes our collective *geulah* — Mashiach ben David. Although Pesach generates the seeds of *geulah* and in many ways brings the redemption to a greater climax, Shavuos offers us the potential to actualize those seedlings and collectively become one by receiving and celebrating the Torah together.

QUESTIONS FOR REFLECTION

- With whom do I feel most comfortable?

- When have I experienced moments of personal redemption?

- What am I doing (if anything) to develop connections between myself and others? Can I be connecting with others better?

10

MENDING THE BROKENNESS: THE THREE WEEKS AND TISHAH B'AV[1]

Rebuilding: the 10th of Teves and the 17th of Tammuz

What does it mean to have walls in life? In truth, we are each vulnerable on some level and need to take measures to protect our inner holiness. Walls protect and establish boundaries, but they can also separate and create barriers between people.

What does it mean to be connected?

The Zohar teaches that the word *kodesh*, holy, can be written with or without a *vav*:

The holiness of connection with a *vav* is holiness manifested within the physical world by people coming together.

There is another type of holiness which is more transcendent than this: *kodesh* without a *vav* is holiness belonging to G-d, which is beyond interpersonal connections.[2]

The political world continuously attempts to build connections. Politicians constantly advise on how various countries or individuals (or groups) ought to unite because it is in their best interest. This is a type of holiness, no doubt, for without people coming together, we would not be able to mend the broken world that we share. This is the paradigm of the leadership of Moses and the revelation of Mount Sinai. It was there that we were taught right from wrong and truth from falsehood, both of which

---

1 Based on the teachings of Reb Shlomo Carlebach as found in Shlomo Katz, ed., *The Soul of Jerusalem: Teachings of Rabbi Shlomo Carlebach* (Mosaica Press, 2015).
2 Katz, *The Soul of Jerusalem*, 144–146.

are essential to achieving social harmony and collective morality.

Still, there is also the leadership of Aaron HaKohen, the High Priest. Aaron was the leader of the Beis HaMikdash, the Holy Temple — a place where the goal was not learning how or when to behave, but rather a place we visited simply to open and pour out our hearts.

This is the holiness of Yerushalayim (Jerusalem). It is connecting beyond connection. We connect not because our judgments tell us that it is better for the both of us overall, but rather because we cannot help but feel a pull toward another's *neshamah*, his soul.

On the level of intellect, we are always protecting ourselves by running away from people and experiences. We escape because it is easier to live a life void of challenges than it is to confront them. Sadly, we always make it a priority to connect with others at the end; we make an effort to show up to a funeral or to sit by someone when he is sick. How often do we exert ourselves to connect for reasons beyond reason, to connect for joyous occasions and to celebrate life together?

As much as these days are set aside to remember the forthcoming destruction of the once-existing Beis HaMikdash, they are wake-up calls for each of us to re-examine the walls we erect in our lives. Are they firm and do they form barriers between ourselves and others, or do they include gates that allow us to connect with the appropriate people at the right times?

Don't wait until the end to connect; we always find reasons why we are too busy in life. Connect now. Connect for no intellectual justification. Connect to holiness because you realize that another has a soul buried deep within, whose root-source you share. And as we piece together our collective soul fragments by uniting with each other, ultimately we can succeed in piecing together the holiness of Yerushalayim.

Seeing the Wholeness within the Brokenness: Tishah b'Av

People can walk the streets of Yerushalayim and see the broken walls, or they can also see the Beis HaMikdash within the walls: within the brokenness. How many of us are broken inside, waiting for others to look at us in the right way? Perhaps more than it is about mourning, Tishah b'Av is about potential. It is about rebuilding; it is about looking at reality and at those around us in the right way: seeing the sweetness within each person. G-d may have destroyed His physical house, but that does not mean that He was not able to envision its eventual rebuilding, to see how holy we would be able to make Yerushalayim at a future time.

Tishah b'Av is about hearing, not seeing. The way we view the world and those around us is based on our own subjectivity and bias. True, we should not ignore that which is in front of us, but how often do we take the time to listen to what our eyes are blind to? How often do we listen to that which is not being said? Reb Shlomo Carlebach teaches that G-d destroyed the Beis HaMikdash because we were only interested in seeing each other and forgot how to listen to one another. Hatred comes from the realm of seeing. It is easy to find fault in others and the wrongs that we perceive they do. But it takes a candle to look into another's soul, and not a beaming torch.[3] The Rabbis teach that the Temple was destroyed because we forgot how to love each other.[4] Yes, Jews may have been learning Torah and acting in accordance with its *mitzvos*, but it seems that sometimes that is not enough.

The 9th of Av is the saddest day of the Jewish calendar, when we sit on the ground and mourn over the loss of G-d's earthly house. But it is through our crying[5] that we remind ourselves how to listen again. When we are faced with darkness and destruction, can we muster up the courage to also see the potential for light and goodness? When we confront a broken world, can we envision its potential for wholeness and work together to transform that dream into a reality? The rebuilding starts now.

---

3   A beaming torch magnifies the faults that we perceive in others because it is so bright. In contrast, a candle is gentler and allows us to see into the crevices of a person's *neshamah*, to discover what is truly buried beneath the *aveiros* (transgressions) we perceive him to be doing.
4   The Rabbis attribute one of the primary causes of the destruction of the Second *Beis HaMikdash* to *sinas chinam*, baseless hatred between people (*Yoma* 9b).
5   The Rabbis teach (*Taanis* 30b) that all those who mourn the destruction of Jerusalem will merit to see its ultimate rejoicing.

QUESTIONS FOR REFLECTION

- What do I cry over?

- What would be (or has been) the greatest loss in my life?

- Do I have too many or too few walls in my life? Are they healthy walls or do they prevent me from excelling?

11

A NEVER-ENDING STORY

Life is a work of art, a huge canvas on which we paint our narratives. Our task is to create our realities, constantly building ourselves as we discover and unlock potentials we never knew we possessed. Just as G-d renews Creation with each passing moment, so too must we constantly be renewing ourselves and never settling for who we think we are at a given point. This is our way of partnering with Him in completing the initial works of Creation.

The journey of potential and the art of self-actualization are immensely personal. Only we can answer our own callings and narrate our own lives. Life is what we choose it to be; it consists of the relationships we choose to form, the growth we choose to make, and the people we choose to transform ourselves into. G-d blesses each of us with the gift of life, but leaves it in each of our hands to bring to fruition as we develop.

Although this book now comes to a close, the ending of my story is only the beginning of your own. The beauty in the journey of self-discovery is that our potential is constantly unfolding. Our stories only come to a close when we each choose to cease authorship. We are each a channel between what was and what can be.

APPENDIX

UNFOLDING FURTHER POTENTIAL

ELUL

Being Human

The totality of the month of Elul encompasses the realization that we are human beings, not angels. For a brief period of time — a mere 30 days — we put aside our "normal" lives and put forth our best efforts to welcome and show honor to a new Guest. *Teshuvah* is not about becoming perfect individuals, for holiness is a journey and not a final destination. *Teshuvah* is the act of setting aside time to remind ourselves that we are on such a journey, and that no matter how ordinary our lives appear throughout the year, we have within us the ability to tap into holiness at moments along the way. Then, after all is said and done, and we return to the lives we had pushed aside, we become better able to glean light from our short visit and use it to illuminate the lives we live day to day.

The Art of Teshuvah

Ani l'dodi v'dodi li — I am to my Beloved as my Beloved is to me.[1] This is what the Rabbis teach is the acronym for the month of Elul, the final month in the Jewish calendar. It is a time of *simchah*, of joy, because it is a type of rebirth, a chance to start afresh. The early generations of Chassidim taught that it is a time when "the King is in the field." They explain this with the following parable:

> All year long, the king of a particular region remains in his castle, overseeing his nation from a distance. Once a year, however, he takes leave of his royal chambers and goes for a stroll amidst his people. Elul is a time to experience a closeness with G-d that may not necessarily be accessible to the same extent during the rest of the year.[2] For 30 days,

---
1 Song of Songs 6:3.
2 *Likkutei Torah, Parshas Re'eh*.

the King comes out to offer a personal invitation to each individual to embark on a new journey together.

People tend to associate the month of Elul with feelings of trepidation. Many view it as a time for repentance over any wrongdoings that may have been committed during the year past. While Elul should certainly be viewed as a serious time, and it is appropriate to review one's actions and priorities throughout the month, it would be wrong to associate the month with judgment alone. Judgment, by nature, focuses on the past: an analysis of what an individual has already done (or not done). While we each must learn from previous actions, Judaism (and by extension, life itself) cannot remain fixated on what has already occurred. Life must be lived in the present, and the choices we each make must be about creating a brighter and more meaningful future.

The Hebrew word commonly used to refer to repentance is *teshuvah*.[3] *Teshuvah*, however, can be understood as two separate words: *tashuv hey* — the returning of the [letter] *hey*.[4] While *teshuvah* is one's personal return to a previous state of being, on a more metaphysical level, it can also be seen as the returning of the letter *hey*. What does this mean? The mystics teach that there are actually two different types of letter *hey*, a symbolically lower one and a higher one: the former of intellect and the latter of action.

G-d's four-letter name is comprised of three different letters: *yud*, *hey*, and *vav* (a final *hey* appears at the end):

- The *yud* is symbolic of a seminal point of inspiration and is likened to *chochmah*, wisdom. In the teachings of Chassidus,[5] the genesis of any idea originates in the realm of *chochmah*; *chochmah* is comprised of the words *koach mah*,[6] the potential of what is, because that concept has not yet been processed and fully actualized.

- The first *hey*, representing the attribute of *binah*, femininity, allows

---

3 By contrast, the word literally means "to return."
4 The Rabbis connect the letter *hey* with the process of *teshuvah* (*Menachos* 29a).
5 Tanya 3.
6 Ibid. 18.

us to begin processing our initial idea. Just as a mother nurtures a child for nine months within her womb, *binah* allows us to process and nurture our ideas: bringing potential into actuality.[7]

- The *vav*, a straight line giving the appearance of a vertical channel, symbolizes the downward journey of bringing abstract (and potentially dangerous) logic into practical and safe reality.

- And the final *hey*, the higher level of *binah*, is a final processing moment in which the thinker transitions into a doer and converts his abstract thoughts into practical actions. The art of *teshuvah* means returning our actions to our thoughts, mending the gap between how we behave and the people we know ourselves capable of being.

As we have seen, Judaism is not interested in our past as much as it is in our present — in the here and now. None of us can perform *mitzvos* in the past, nor can we alter or erase what has already taken place at a particular time. At best, each of us can focus on the resources we currently possess and places in which we find ourselves and ask how we can transform our potentials into reality. The month of Elul is not about sadness. It is about becoming whole again, becoming more than we once were. *Teshuvah* is not about returning to where we were prior to slipping, but rather, about returning to the state of existence in which we *could* have been prior to whichever mistake we made.

Ani l'dodi v'dodi li is written in the present tense, because it is not about what we *did*, but about what we *can do*; not who we *were*, but who we *can become*; not about remaining stuck in our past (our subconscious selves), but about actively pursuing the tomorrow we so desire.

---

7   Ibid. 2, 3.

The King has taken leave of His palace. The gates of *teshuvah* are open. The time is now, and the place is here. The journey has begun, but it is up to each of us to decide whether we want to actualize ourselves or not, whether we want to remain the same or act different today than we did yesterday.

SIMCHAS TORAH

To Dance as a Jew

Why do we dance in circles?

We dance in circles because no one person is better than another; no one is in the first or last row, or at either end of a line.

We dance in circles because the totality of life consists of a large circle: each time we reach a particular point, we approach it more elevated and with a new awareness than we did previously, only to encounter it again in the near or distant future.

We dance in circles because a square represents four corners of confinement. A circle, by contrast, consists of a continuous line: an endless journey with infinite potentials waiting to unfold. When we run, although we may progress forward, we do so linearly and as individuals. When we dance, however, we move together, each one uplifting the other.

CHANUKAH

Zos Chanukah

The Rabbis teach[8] that it would be fitting for us to build a *sukkah* large enough to house every single Jew.

What if we were to build a menorah that contained enough branches to kindle the spark of G-d buried within each of our *neshamos*, our souls? The final day of Chanukah is referred to as *Zos Chanukah, This is Chanukah*[9] — but why? Don't the previous seven days merit any special mention? Why is only this one day referred to as *Zos Chanukah*?

The holiday of Chanukah is all about transcendence. The Sages of Beis Hillel instruct that when involving ourselves in matters of holiness, our only avenue therein is to increase from what has already been done.[10] Whereby the number seven is a representation of the consistency and confinement of the laws of nature,[11] the number eight symbolizes the breaking free of that confinement. We kindle a total of eight lights on Chanukah because the flames are meant to teach us that there is more to life than the consistency of the laws of nature and the realm of logic. Within the realm of the intellect, it is easy to judge others, and oftentimes ourselves. Living in a world of the number seven, it is easy to find fault within others and the reality in which we live. The Chanukah lights teach us that there is so much more to life than what our eyes first take notice of, and there is so much more to our initial judgments of others. Only by adopting the mentality of the number eight can we overcome our differences and unite as a people.

---

8   *Sukkah* 27b.
9   Taken from the Torah reading for that day, which includes the words, *"zos hamizbei'ach"* (Numbers 7:54–8:4).
10 The Sages of Beis Hillel and Beis Shammai debate whether the Chanukah lights must be kindled in ascending or descending order throughout the eight days of the holiday (*Shabbos* 21a).
11 As the natural world was created within a total of seven days.

Olive Oil: Facts and Their Lessons

1. Oil can only be produced from pressing olives: it must be humbled before it can become pure.

   To achieve greatness in life, we must first learn to master the art of humility: we must realize our worth even when crushed. Growth only occurs after acknowledging our mistakes and learning from them as we journey through our lives.

2. Oil penetrates almost all surfaces: once oil comes into contact with something, it leaves a lasting impression.

   Our task in life is not just to inspire ourselves, but also to inspire others. In order to connect with another, we must share a part of ourselves — our souls — that are much deeper than the physical surface of reality. Like oil, we must strive to leave a positive and lasting impression on anyone we encounter.

3. Oil does not mix with other liquids: oil will always remain distinct and rise to the top of any mixture regardless of how much that mixture has been blended.

   No matter how humble or how inspiring we become, we can never let that prevent us from remaining (and further becoming) unique individuals — each having something special to offer humanity. Like oil, we can never allow ourselves to lose our own identity and assume that of another. When we approach others with humbleness and genuineness, we cannot help but rise to the top — not because we are any more holy than them, but because we understand that each rises up together, each helping the other become more whole.

Three More Lessons Learned from the Chanukah Lights

1. We must constantly be adding more light to our lives as the days pass

by. Life is not about being content with who we are at a given moment, but rather about always striving to become more tomorrow than we were today. Life is about continued growth, not about stagnation.

2. Each night we are only allowed to add one additional flame regardless of how motivated we feel that day — growth is not about making big changes right away because we experience jolts of inspiration, but rather about making small and impactful changes that are lasting.

3. Though we start with only one small flame, we know that in the end we will ultimately ignite all eight — success may seem like it takes a lifetime to attain, but in the end we know we will achieve it...for each small success, each tiny light that we add to our existing flame, amounts to a sacred fire that we can use to light up ourselves and the world around us.

PESACH

Understanding the "Wicked" Child

Who is the *rasha*, the so-called "wicked" child that asks the second of the four questions on Seder Night? Is he truly so different from the *chacham*, the "wise" child, who begins the questioning? Essentially, both children ask about the *mitzvos* and both direct their questions not at themselves, but to the one answering.

What the "wicked" child does on Seder Night, explains Rebbe Nachman,[12] is that he makes a mockery of Judaism. Still, deep within, the "wicked" child belittles Judaism as a way of coping with his frustration at the discrepancy between the self we portray him as and the self he knows he is capable of becoming if only we encouraged him to actualize himself. He is a child who is no less holy than his seemingly "wise" sibling, but perhaps we never took the time to show him how much he mattered. Perhaps we never told him how holy he was.[13]

Quite possibly, this is why the author of the Haggadah emphasizes the "wicked" child's question as one of separation: "What is this service to *you*? To you and not to him. And by so doing, he removes himself from the collective..." Because he views himself as different from everyone else, the "wicked" child spends his days analyzing others and fails to see his own self-worth and holiness embedded within. When measured against his three other siblings, he sees himself as a sinner and a failure. But what might happen if he compared himself only to himself?

Could it be that the "wicked" child immediately follows his "wise" sibling in the context of the Haggadah narrative as a way of teaching us that there is a grave danger in being *too* wise, too intellectual? Reb Shlomo

---

12 Yehoshua Starret, compiler, Moshe Mykoff, ed., Chaim Kramer, trans., *The Breslov Haggadah* (Jerusalem/New York: Breslov Research Institute, 1989).
13 Chaim Stefansky, ed., *The Carlebach Haggadah* (Jerusalem: Urim Publications, 2001).

Carlebach teaches[14] that this is the reason why the Haggadah instructs us to educate the "wise" child about all of Judaism's *mitzvos* until the very last detail of the *Afikoman* — because Judaism is much more than a pursuit of intellectuality and a series of commands that we are instructed to follow. Indeed, the *mitzvos* are fundamental to how we ought to conduct ourselves, but if we are unable to taste the "sweetness" therein, we run the risk of losing our connectedness and passion for continuity.

In truth, each of us possesses fragments of potential waiting to be actualized and allowed to surface. Although the "wise" child is praised for his intellectual thirst, because he is still just a child, he cannot yet foresee the consequences of not balancing his curiosity and drive for knowledge with an emotional connection to Judaism. The "wicked" child will forever remain suffocating within the confines of Egypt unless he becomes willing to envision an identity for himself that is separate from the one we constantly portray him as having each year. Both children run the risk of remaining enslaved: the "wise" child to intellectual dryness and the "wicked" child to his negative and damaging perceptions about his own identity.

The "wicked" child must realize that he was not created to be the *tzaddik*, the righteous individual, he judges his (seemingly) older sibling to be; he was created to be himself — to be the fullest and truest self possible. Perhaps he secretly knows this, but behaves as he does because it is easier to live under an identity that others thrust upon us than it is to live with one that we create on our own.

The "wicked" child lacks the courage to be holy because he senses that we have given up on him. He comes to Seder Night each year and continues to question, continues longing for positive encouragement. Will we grant him his deserved empowerment this year or will we cast him off as a "wicked" child once again, only partaking of the festivities for a free meal?

Seder Night offers some of the greatest opportunities for achieving unity: unity of our people, unity of several generations, unity within our own selves, and beyond all, unity between heaven and earth. We may each speak different languages or have distinct family customs, but we are all still part of the same people.

---

14 Ibid.

Together, we will encounter four unique children, four young individuals longing to be a part of something much larger than their individual selves. They come each year, but that does not mean that we should be judging them on the same grounds as we have in years past. Today we are here, tomorrow we can choose to come closer to the selves we are capable of being. This year we are "here"; next year may we merit to unite in the Holy Land of Eretz Yisrael!

PESACH SHEINI

It's Never Too Late

Exactly one year following the Exodus from Egypt, the Jews were commanded to celebrate Pesach, but a select few who had become *tamei*[15] could not participate. They protested to Moses: Why should they be excluded from participation in holiness on these grounds alone? Surely they should be given another opportunity on a later date once they had rectified themselves.

Pesach Sheini, the Second Pesach, is all about second chances. A second chance is an understanding that life is a journey of continued growth, that one ought never remain in the same place, but continuously trek forward across his lifespan. It is the realization that, in the words of the Chassidic masters, every descent is, essentially, the preparation for an ascent. There is really no such thing as falling off course as long as we choose to pick ourselves up thereafter and continue our journey.

King Solomon – the wisest of all men – writes[16] that a *tzaddik* can fall seven times before rising up one final time. But how can a righteous person fall? The Baal HaTanya teaches[17] that in order to qualify as a complete *tzaddik* (righteous individual), we must not only convert our animalistic qualities into holy expressions, but we must completely eradicate any trace of evil from within ourselves to the point where we no longer derive any form of pleasure from the material world in which we live. How could it be possible for a *tzaddik* to even fall once, let alone seven times?!

If a *tzaddik* cannot fall from the onset, how could King Solomon encourage him to pick himself up thereafter? Perhaps it would be easiest to imagine a sequence of platforms. When King Solomon teaches that a

---

15 A state of ritual impurity that one enters by coming in contact with the dead (oftentimes against his will).
16 Proverbs 24:16.
17 Tanya 10.

tzaddik falls seven times, could it be that he implies a transition from one platform to the next instead of a literal descent? Akin to a graduate of primary school entering secondary school, the "fall" is not truly a descent, but rather a period of transition between one state of reality and a higher rung of living.

A *tzaddik* understands that life is a series of continuous growth. Demanding a second chance at holiness means never being content with, or settling for, the platform on which we find ourselves, but always striving to reach new heights and overcome new challenges.

ABOUT THE AUTHOR

Jonah S.C. Muskat-Brown is a licensed and registered social worker from the Greater Toronto Area. He draws inspiration from a broad scope of Torah sources and professional theorists, and utilizes both to see the inherent worth in each individual. He is passionate about breaking down barriers between people, and strives to inspire others to become their fullest selves possible. He can be contacted via LinkedIn.

ABOUT MOSAICA PRESS

Mosaica Press is an independent publisher of Jewish books. Our authors include some of the most profound, interesting, and entertaining thinkers and writers in the Jewish community today. There is a great demand for high-quality Jewish works dealing with issues of the day — and Mosaica Press is helping fill that need. Our books are available around the world. Please visit us at **www.mosaicapress.com** or contact us at **info@mosaicapress.com**. We will be glad to hear from you.